GOD'S PEOPLE: OUR STORY

God's People: Our Story

Bible Stories
from the New Testament

DeVere Ramsay

Illustrations by
Francis Huffman

THE UPPER ROOM
Nashville, Tennessee

God's People: Our Story

Book design: Harriette Bateman
First Printing: June 1984 (10)
Library of Congress Catalog Card Number: 84-51404
ISBN: 0-8358-0480-1

Printed in the United States of America

Dedicated to my husband,

William M. Ramsay,

with love and devotion,
without whose help this
book could not have been written.

Contents

Preface

This is a book of twelve stories about Jesus. But it also tells *one story*: what the life of Jesus is all about.

The stories are about different people and the way they responded to Jesus. So it is also a story about you and me.

All these stories come from the New Testament. Most of the characters appear in scripture. Some do not have names in the Bible, so I have given them names to help make the truth of the stories more vivid.

For example, the New Testament tells us that religious leaders known as Pharisees and Sadducees opposed Jesus. I have simply given the names "Nathan" and "Eli" to two of them to represent the others. There really was a secret gang known as Zealots plotting revolution in the time of Jesus. I have called one of these men "Isaac." (Another Zealot, Barabbas, actually appears in the Gospel narrative.) The Bible tells us that a young girl accused Peter of being a disciple the night Jesus was on trial. I have given her the name "Tamar." We do not know whether she later became a Christian, but I have let her represent what really did happen to many boys and girls after the Holy Spirit came at Pentecost.

In every case where I have used imagination in this way, I have done so simply to present more dramatically the truth just as it is found in the New Testament.

Contemporary thinkers are emphasizing that the Bible presents theology through stories. *Theology* is the study of ideas of the kind with which this book deals. How does the story of Jesus build on the Old Testament? What are some of the important ideas that Jesus taught? How is Christmas related to Good Friday? Why did Jesus die? What did Jesus mean when he talked about the kingdom of God? What kind of changes does the Holy Spirit make in people's lives? What is required of people when they become followers of Jesus? This book tries to answer questions like these *through stories* in ways that are simple enough for children to understand.

Indeed, in large part it is by telling stories that the New Testament has come to us. Christians told each other stories, and parents told stories to their children long before any of the New Testament was written. It was probably more than thirty years after Easter before the first Gospel came into being. But the stories of Jesus were preserved because people loved him and wanted to tell each other about him. This book seeks to recapture the excitement of the spirit of those early days of the church.

Preface

In retelling these New Testament stories I have made use of what has seemed to me the best contemporary interpretation in the light of the teachings of the church through the centuries. Every effort has been made to reflect accurately the history of New Testament times.

But these are not just stories of long ago. As you read, I hope you will see yourself imaginatively in every story and that you will become aware of what being a follower of Jesus can mean for you today.

—DeVere Ramsay

Chapter 1

A King Is Born

Jonathan wriggled closer to the campfire. It was a cold night but clear, and the warmth of the fire felt good to the young shepherd boy.

Jonathan liked to hear the grown-up shepherds talk and tell stories each night around the campfire. He especially liked to hear about David. His favorite story was the one about David killing a giant!

"I never saw the stars so bright," said Laban, Jonathan's grandfather, as he looked up into the moonless sky. "It must have been nights such as this that King David used to enjoy as a boy keeping sheep on this same Bethlehem hillside."

"Someday God's people will have a new king like David," added Boaz, one of the other shepherds. "Yes, someday our Messiah will come and set God's people free."

The sheep that Jonathan and the other shepherds raised were special sheep. They were the ones that would be sold in Jerusalem to be used in Temple sacrifices. They must be perfect sheep, strong and healthy and beautiful. Jonathan helped his grandfather give the lambs the best possible care. He heard a wolf howl in the distance, reminding him that wild animals were never far away. He knew their lambs and sheep were safe, though. He fingered his own sling. To protect the sheep he would kill a wolf himself if he had to.

The shepherds were still talking as Jonathan fell asleep. As Jonathan became drowsy, he half heard one of them say something about the prophets of old who had foretold the coming of a Messiah.

"Yes," the shepherd said, "God's people have a hope that one day a new king will come and will set us free."

Suddenly Jonathan was wide awake. There was a bright light all around him. He sat up and rubbed his eyes. He was very scared—and so were all the other shepherds. They heard a voice that said:

"Don't be afraid. I bring you good news that will be to all people. For to you is born this day in the city of David a Savior, who is Christ the Lord. And this will be a sign for you: you will find a babe wrapped in swaddling cloths and lying in a manger."

To Jonathan's surprise the whole sky was now filled with a heavenly choir singing,

> Glory to God in the highest,
> and on earth, peace.

Then . . . silence. All was quiet once more. Only the stars twinkled in the midnight sky.

The shepherds jumped to their feet. "Our Savior has come!" Boaz shouted.

"A new king—a king like David. He will set us free!" exclaimed one of the shepherds. "Christ the Lord has been born."

"We must go find this baby," said Boaz. "He is our king. We must go to Bethlehem, the city where David was born. Let's go and worship our king."

"We can't all go," cautioned Laban. "I will stay here and watch the sheep. Jonathan, go with the others. You can tell me all about the baby when you come back."

As the shepherds and the boy made their way toward Bethlehem, they wondered where to look for the baby. "How will we find the child?" Boaz asked as he led the group across the hillside.

"The angel said we would find the baby in a manger," Jonathan reminded them. The other shepherds laughed.

"Why a manger is a box where animals eat," chuckled Boaz as he put his hand on Jonathan's shoulder. "No king would have a manger for a cradle."

As they came into town, they passed a group of Roman soldiers patrolling the streets. Soldiers were always on duty.

"Halt!" shouted one of them. "Where are you going at this hour of the night?"

"We are looking for a baby—a very special baby," Boaz answered.

The soldier put his hands on his hips and

laughed loudly. He said to himself, *How can a baby be special? These shepherds and the boy look harmless enough. No baby could be a threat to Rome.* One more look at them and he let them pass.

The shepherds rushed down the cobblestone street of the darkened city. Not knowing where to begin looking for the child, the shepherds went to the inn, encouraged by seeing a light there.

"Open up!" Boaz spoke, pounding on the door. "Open the door. We have a question."

"Go away," shouted the innkeeper from inside. "We have no more rooms. We have been turning people away since five o'clock. We are tired. My family and I are in bed."

"I don't want a room. We are looking for a baby that has just been born. Do you happen to know . . . ?"

The innkeeper's wife had heard the confusion and came and opened the door. "A baby?" she asked. She spoke in a more friendly way than had her husband. "Yes, there was a couple here about supper time who were expecting a baby. We had no room here in the inn, but we told them they could sleep in our stable if they wanted to. To me, that poor, weary young woman looked as if the baby might be born any minute."

"Thank you for the information," the shepherds responded.

"In the stable!"shouted Jonathan. "That must be where the baby is. The angel said we would find the baby lying in a manger. And in the stable there will be a manger."

In excitement the shepherds ran toward the courtyard of the inn. There in the stable they found the usual assortment of animals—donkeys, cows, a few sheep. A woman and a man were there—and in the manger, a tiny baby.

The shepherds stood in wonder at what they saw. It was just as the angel had told them!

"Come, see my baby," said the mother. Her name was Mary. She was seated beside the manger on a pile of hay. She picked up the baby and held him tenderly. Her husband Joseph moved closer. The shepherds crowded around them. To see the baby better, Jonathan got on his knees and inched closer. He timidly reached out and patted the baby. The mother smiled.

Boaz and the others told Mary and Joseph what had happened on the hillside. They told of the angel and the heavenly song.

"An angel spoke to me, too," responded Joseph. "He told me we would call the baby 'Jesus,' for he will save God's people from their sins."

As the shepherds left the stable, their voices were raised in songs of praise.

"Make a joyful noise unto the Lord," they sang. "Come before his presence with singing!" They told all they met that Christ the Lord had been born.

Rejoicing, the shepherds returned to Laban and their sheep. Jonathan was excited. He wanted to be the first to tell Laban the good news. "Grandfather," he exclaimed, "we found the baby! Our Savior has been born!" The shepherds said, "It's true. We found him lying in a manger in the stable at the inn. His name is Jesus, and he will save people from their sins."

About forty days later, Laban said to Jonathan, "I must go to Jerusalem, my boy, and I would like for you to go with me. I must make a delivery of some of our lambs to the Temple. I could use your help."

"Oh, yes, Grandfather," replied Jonathan with excitement. This was the first time he had ever been allowed to go on such an important mission. "Yes! I would like to help you take the lambs to the Temple."

As Jonathan and Laban came into the Temple area with their lambs, the boy felt sad. He knew the moment had come when he would have to part with the little animals he had helped raise. He kept looking at them as Laban made the sale, received his money, and turned the lambs over to the merchants who would sell them for sacrificing.

As Jonathan and Laban were still in the court-yard, Jonathan pulled at Laban's sleeve. "Grandfather! Grandfather!" he almost yelled. "Look!" he pointed. "See that man and woman over there going into the Temple—the ones with the baby? I'm sure they are the man and woman I saw in the stable in Bethlehem the night the baby was born."

"Yes, I see them, Jonathan. And since we are

here at the Temple, let's go in ourselves for a few minutes."

Inside the Temple, Laban and Jonathan saw an old, old man (Simeon was his name) stop the family, take the baby in his arms, and in a hoarse, unsteady voice begin to sing:

> With my eyes
> I have seen salvation.
> This child will bring glory
> to all God's people everywhere.

Jonathan pulled at Laban's robe again. "Grandfather," he whispered this time. "What that old man said sounded a lot like what the angels told us the night that baby was born!"

"So it does, my boy," replied his grandfather.

They watched as an old woman now came toward the baby.

"See that old woman?" Laban whispered. "She's been coming here faithfully since I was your age. Her name is Anna. She keeps hoping to see the Messiah."

The stooped, wrinkled woman now looked at the baby a long time and bowed her head in silent prayer. As she lifted her head she called in a loud voice, "This child will grow up to set God's people free."

Jonathan and his grandfather left the Temple. As they walked through the streets, they thought of all they had seen and heard that day and in the days before.

"Perhaps," said Laban, as he placed his hand on Jonathan's shoulder, "this child really is our new king, our Messiah we have hoped for all these years. He could indeed be God's son who will save us from our sins and set all God's people free."

Chapter 2

A Trip to the Temple

In his home in Nazareth, Jesus lay very still on his bed. Most of the town was still asleep. The boy, however, was already awake. He was listening for the faithful family rooster to announce the dawn.

Jesus' mind was filled with questions. *What will it be like to celebrate Passover in the Temple of Jerusalem?* he thought. *Now that I am twelve years old, I will be able to worship God in the Temple itself!*

Jesus had been to the Temple before. He was only a tiny baby, then, however, brought there by Mary and Joseph. Now, of course, he could not remember that. All his life he had heard stories about Jerusalem and the Temple. At last he was really going there.

The rooster crowed.

He heard shuffling feet on the lower level of the cottage. Mary, his mother, was awake, too—and already busy with preparations for the trip. Jesus could smell the fire and hear it crackling.

The boy jumped to his feet and began to roll up his pallet bed.

"Jesus, are you awake?" His mother had heard him. "Your father needs you to help load the donkey."

"Coming, Mother. I'm almost ready." The boy's heart was pounding as he put finishing touches on his bedroll.

"Have I forgotten anything?" he wondered. He spotted his ball and added it to his pack.

Joseph was loading the small donkey as Mary carried bundles of food and cooking utensils to be tied to the animal's back.

"Give me a hand with the cord on the other side," Joseph said to Jesus as the boy put his own bedroll on the ground and helped. "And now get my saw from the carpenter bench. We'll need it to cut firewood along the way." The boy dashed back into the cottage and brought the tool. His mother joined them with one more sack of grain.

"I'm glad you are old enough now to go with us to the Temple, Jesus," she chattered as she checked to be sure she had everything she would need for cooking. "Your cousin John and his mother Elizabeth will join the caravan as we pass through the Judean hill country. I am so fond of Elizabeth. She's an old woman now and this may well be the last year she will be able to make the trip. I've told you many times what she meant to me just before you were born. John is just about your age—only six months older. You two will have a good time together on the trip."

Joseph gave one last tug on the baggage cord and gave the donkey a gentle pat. "There now, small one,

with your help I believe we should have a good trip. We'll join the rest of the caravan at the edge of town."

It seemed everybody in Jesus' hometown of Nazareth was going to the feast this year—everybody, that is, except Jesus' younger brothers and sisters. Arrangements had been made for them to stay behind with an older aunt as Jesus himself had often done. But other aunts were going, and uncles and cousins and several of Jesus' friends from the synagogue school. Jesus was now a part of the "grown people" of the town. It was exciting to be twelve years old at last!

It was a long way from Nazareth to Jerusalem—about one hundred miles. It would take four days and three nights. Jesus wondered why the trip had to take so long. As the family made its way down the narrow street, the boy ran ahead to fall in step with Joseph.

"Tell me," he said as he tried to keep up with Joseph's long stride. "Why do we have to travel such a long way around to get to Jerusalem? Darius, the camel driver with the merchant's caravan, told me just last week that there is a much shorter way to go. His caravan goes down the west of the Jordan River instead of along the east bank. They have to go through Samaria, of course, but. . . ."

"Ah, yes, my son," Joseph interrupted. "But Jews try not to travel through Samaria. The route we will travel is longer, but it is the way we must go."

Jesus did not reply. He stopped beside the village well to draw a jug of water. He wondered to himself about the bad feelings between the Samaritans and Jews. He poured the water into a wineskin and tucked it under his arm.

As the family joined the others, the caravan slowly made its way down the rocky road. Some people rode on donkeys. A rich family had brought their camel. Most people walked. Little children had to be carried. But Jesus and the older children ran and skipped along the road.

They traveled all morning. They traveled all afternoon. When twilight came they waded across the Jordan River and built a campfire on the bank on the other side. There they cooked their supper over the burning coals and ate it under the trees.

Until bedtime the group sat around the campfire

telling stories and singing psalms in praise of God. The older folk told of things that had happened when they were young. Sometimes they told stories of what God had done for the Hebrew people many years before. They talked of the first Passover and how God, through Moses, had delivered the Israelites out of the land of Egypt.

Some of the children fell asleep as they listened to the stories. By midnight all the people had spread their bedrolls on the soft grass and were asleep beneath the stars.

When morning came the journey began again. They passed Mount Tabor and went through the valley where, centuries before, Deborah, the woman judge, had helped lead her army to victory. The caravan traveled beside the river, where flowers were blooming in all their springtime color. But later they had to trudge through barren desert country where hot sand ground into their sandaled feet.

As they traveled the next two days, they often saw groups of Roman soldiers patrolling the highway. They were reminded that the Jews were a people who were not really free. One man spat and shook his fist at the back of a passing Roman centurion.

They crossed the Jordan River once more. They came near the ruins of the fortress of Jericho. Joseph put his arm around Jesus' shoulder. "Remember the story I have told you about Joshua and the time the walls of Jericho fell?" he said. "Look at that hill over there. Those are the remains of that old fort. God

gave the Hebrews the victory. Our God is one who takes care of God's own people."

Now the group began to climb a mountain so high the boys and girls found themselves panting for breath at every step. Someone started singing, "I will lift up my eyes to the hills," and all joined in singing the psalm. As they sang, at last in the distance Jesus saw Jerusalem! And on a hill in the city he could see the Temple.

By this time the caravan that had left Nazareth four days earlier had been joined by hundreds of other people who were also going to Jerusalem to celebrate Passover. It was the largest crowd that Jesus had ever seen. "Just think," the boy said softly, "they are all going to Jerusalem to worship God!"

As they entered the city, Jesus, his family, and all the others crowded through the huge stone gate in the big stone wall. They walked up the hill. Step by step they climbed. At the very top of the hill they came to the white marble Temple, glistening in the bright spring sunshine.

The crowd now climbed the broad stone steps. They entered the Temple through the golden doors. They stood inside the marble walls. Now Jesus could smell the burning sacrifices and hear the Temple choir. Suddenly the silver trumpet sounded its call to worship.

Mary stopped in the court of the women, but Jesus joined Joseph and the other men in the great Temple. There they stood and sang praise and said prayers to God. There teachers taught them about God's love. "O give thanks to the Lord, for he is good." Jesus joined in the chorus. "His steadfast love endures forever!"

Finally it was time to go back to Nazareth. The caravan started for home.

About dinner time Mary said to Joseph, "I wonder where Jesus is. I haven't seen him since we left Jerusalem."

"Come to think of it, I haven't seen him either. I suppose he is up ahead of us with some of the other boys and girls."

"Let's be sure, Joseph. It would be terrible if we left him behind."

Mary and Joseph hurried back and forth asking for Jesus. No one had seen him.

"Oh, Joseph," sobbed Mary. "He isn't with the caravan. We must have left him behind in Jerusalem. How could we have done that? I thought he left the Temple when we did. I never dreamed he wasn't with some of his friends."

"There, there, Mary," comforted Joseph as he put his strong arm around her. "We'll go back to Jerusalem and find him."

They turned around and almost ran back to the city. They entered again through the large stone gate. They raced up the hill. Again they entered the great golden doors of the Temple.

And there they found Jesus—talking with the teachers. He was asking the learned men questions. And Jesus was answering questions the learned men were asking him.

"Jesus, Jesus," cried his mother. "At last we have found you! But why in the world have you done this to us? Your father and I have been looking for you for three hours. We thought we'd never find you. You should have known how worried we would be."

"You shouldn't have worried, Mother," the boy gently replied. "Didn't you know that I would be in my Father's house? I have been here all the time. I have been talking with the teachers and learning about God."

"It is time to go home now though," said Mary lovingly.

With his mother's arm around him, Jesus and his family left the Temple and went home to Nazareth together.

There at home with his family and friends Jesus grew to be strong and tall. But he grew in other ways, too. He studied hard. He learned to be a good carpenter as he helped Joseph in the shop. He learned a lot when he was by himself.

Often he sat beneath a tree on a hillside near Nazareth and just thought and prayed. As he watched merchant caravans pass by, he remembered his own trip to Jerusalem. He thought of things that had happened on that journey and of things he had learned. That trip to the Temple when he was twelve years old helped Jesus learn more about God's love and about God's people. Events around him were helping to shape his life. Jesus was beginning to understand something of what his calling was to be. The child was becoming an adult.

Chapter 3

A Servant King

Sabbath service had ended. Jesus and other men of Nazareth were gathered on the synagogue steps. Reuben and Caleb were telling of their trip to the Dead Sea region to hear John the Baptizer.

"I think the man is crazy," said Caleb. "Nobody in his right mind would live in the desert and eat only grasshoppers and wild honey."

"He's not crazy, Caleb. He's a prophet. He was preaching about the kingdom of God. Remember, the Baptizer quoted some of the same scriptures we heard read tonight in the service."

The scripture that night had been a passage from the prophet Isaiah. The rabbi had opened the large scroll, seated himself before the congregation, and read:

> Someone is shouting in the desert
> "Get the road ready for the Lord;
> Make a straight path for him to travel."

The desert preacher that they talked about was Jesus' first cousin. Jesus had not seen him for a long

32

time. *So that is what John said,* Jesus thought. *I wonder what else he preaches.*

The women and girls who had been at the service were interested in the conversation the men were having and tried to listen to what was said. It bothered Jesus that men and women had to sit separately in the synagogue service, and even after the service the women stood apart.

"Hundreds of people were out there in that barren countryside listening to John the Baptizer," Reuben continued. "He told people to stop doing wrong. They were to feed the hungry and give clothes to any who needed them. He said we must all be honest. He called on us all to repent and be baptized."

"Some said he was the Messiah, but I surely don't think so," interrupted Caleb.

"I heard him say," Reuben went on with his story, "that someone is coming who is greater than he. 'I baptize with water, but he will baptize with the Holy Spirit,' he said. I don't know what he meant."

"God's people have been looking for the Messiah for so many years," one of the other men said with excitement. "Maybe now he has come! Perhaps John is the one who is to bring in the kingdom of God."

As the group broke up, Jesus walked toward his home alone. He was usually surrounded by a crowd of children. Everyone loved him. But tonight he needed to be by himself to think. On his way, he stopped beside the road and sat down on a low wall.

I want to hear John myself, he thought, as he

picked up a stone and tossed it across the road. *Maybe I should be preaching the way John is preaching.*

Jesus had been working as the village carpenter since Joseph had died some years before. As the oldest son in the family, he felt it was his responsibility to care for his mother and his younger brothers and sisters. But now Jesus was thirty years old. His brothers and sisters had all married and now had families of their own.

The word about John the Baptizer that I heard tonight helps me know what I must do, thought Jesus. *As soon as Sabbath is over, I will make arrangements for leaving Mother in the care of my brothers. They can handle the carpenter shop. Yes,* he thought, *I will go to the desert and find my cousin John.*

When Jesus had crossed the rocky desert area to the riverside oasis where John the Baptizer was preaching, he found a large crowd of people. Men, women, and children from all over Palestine had come to hear him. There were rich people, poor people, soldiers, politicians, as well as religious leaders.

Jesus was amazed at the way his cousin looked. Although John was the son of a priest, he certainly didn't look like one. He had long, matted black hair and a thick, dirty beard. He wore a camel skin for his clothes. He was very thin. *A diet of only grasshoppers and wild honey, which is all he could find in the desert, would make anyone thin*, laughed Jesus.

"Turn from doing wrong and be baptized!" John shouted.

A merchant dressed in silk with a fat purse at his belt came to John. "What must I do?" he asked.

John answered, "You are a rich man. Others are poor. Give some of your money to feed hungry people. Repent, I say, and be baptized." The rich man waded with John into the Jordan river and was baptized.

A man in a Roman army uniform with a sword strapped to his side came to him and said, "What about me?"

The Baptizer replied, "Soldier, don't try to take money from people by force. Be satisfied with what you are paid. If you are willing to change your ways, you can be baptized." The soldier went with John into the river.

A politician came to him and said, "What about me?"

The Baptizer replied, "Be honest. This is what God intends for you to do." The politician was baptized.

Nathan, a religious leader, came next. He was dressed in a robe with a long tassel and fringe that showed he was a Pharisee. On his forehead he wore a little box that had in it a scripture verse. He wanted to show everyone that he always had God's word "on his mind."

"What about me?" asked Nathan. "What must I do? After all, I am descended from Abraham. I keep the law of Moses. Surely I have no sins of which I must repent."

A Servant King

"You snake," shouted John the Baptizer. "Who told you that you could escape punishment? You think that because you are a religious leader it doesn't matter how you treat other people. It is time you began to practice what you preach. You must live a good life as well as talk about it. You must. . . ."

Nathan turned and stormed away as John talked. He was certainly not going to be baptized after talk like *that*.

Jesus listened and wondered, *What will John the Baptizer say to me?* He elbowed his way through the crowd and walked toward John. He wanted to be baptized, too.

As John saw Jesus coming, he stopped his preaching. He stood in silence and looked at Jesus. And then he said in a loud voice, "This is the Lamb of God who takes away the sins of the world."

What did John mean? Jesus wondered. He walked into the water with John and was baptized. As he came up the bank, the Holy Spirit came upon him. He heard a voice saying, "This is my beloved Son in whom I am well pleased."

God's Son, thought Jesus. *That is what the psalmist called the promised king. Am I to be the promised king? Am I to bring in God's kingdom? Those other words are from Isaiah*, he remembered. *They are about God's servant— God's suffering servant. Is the voice telling me that I am the promised Messiah? Or am I to be the one who is to suffer for God?*

Jesus had to think. He felt he needed to pray. He

must try to find answers to his questions, to know God's will. He went to a lonely part of the desert. There were no trees — only scrubby bushes and barren rocks. The only sounds were the roar of a lion in the distance and the howl of a wolf at night.

"Turn stones into bread." It was almost as though a voice had spoken to him. "With all these stones, you'd be richer than that rich merchant. And you could feed the world."

"Let people crown you king," the voice within his own mind seemed to say. "There are people in Palestine ready to follow you in leading a revolt. With their help, you could conquer those Roman soldiers, free God's people, and set up your kingdom everywhere.

"Better yet," the inner voice tempted him again. "Go to the Temple itself and jump off the rooftop. God's angels will come and protect you. Then even Nathan and the other religious leaders would believe."

None of these answers seemed right. "Those are not the ways that God means to bring in the kingdom. Go away, Satan," Jesus shouted. He was convinced an evil spirit had been tempting him.

For forty days Jesus struggled with these and other questions. He had been tempted to choose the easy answers. But he knew he could not compromise.

In new ways Jesus began to understand that he was, indeed, the promised Messiah. He was the *king* that God's people had been hoping for. He was to

work to bring about God's kingdom. But he must do it by being God's *servant*. His life must be one of service and sacrifice for others. The kingdom of God was one in which others must be servants, too.

Jesus was filled with the Holy Spirit as he left the desert. He understood and accepted his mission—even if he would be killed for doing it. He knew God wanted him to teach and preach. He knew he must heal the sick. He must help *all* people—poor people, rich people, men, women, boys, and girls.

One week later Jesus was standing on a busy street corner in the city of Capernaum by the Sea of Galilee. He had left the wilderness behind, but he had left his hometown of Nazareth, too. Busy merchants, housewives carrying water home from the well, fishermen on their way to their boats at the water's edge, blind men begging for money, boys and girls at play crowded past him. These and others like them were the ones he had come to serve. Jesus was ready now to begin his ministry to God's people.

Chapter 4

Calling God's People to Serve

"The kingdom of God is near," Jesus proclaimed. "Repent and believe the Good News."

Jesus had been going all over the region of Galilee with the same message. People listened. Crowds began to follow him. He taught. He healed. His mission was beginning.

One day he came to the town of Capernaum. "Come here," he called to two fishermen as he walked along the beach beside the Sea of Galilee. "Come, follow me," he said. "I need your help." One of the men was Andrew. The other was his brother Simon. The men waded to shore from their fishing boat and sat down on the sand beside Jesus.

"Simon," said Jesus, "I am going to give you a new name. I'm going to call you 'Peter,' which means 'rock.' You will become strong like a rock. From now on you will be my rock." Peter was puzzled, but he was pleased with the new name.

Other boats filled the lake. One was larger and finer than all the rest.

"That boat," explained Peter, "belongs to Zebedee and his sons, James and John. They are sometimes called 'Sons of Thunder.' They salt the fish they catch and sell it as far south as Jerusalem. I understand they have relatives who are members of the High Court."

"Call them over," said Jesus. "I'd like to meet them."

Andrew rose and walked close to the water's edge and called, "James, John, here is someone we'd like for you to meet."

The "Sons of Thunder" joined the others on the shore. They were younger than Peter and Andrew. John, in fact, was still in his early teens.

"We'd like for you to meet Jesus," Andrew said as he introduced them. "He is a teacher from Nazareth."

"I need your help," Jesus said. "Come, follow me."

There was something about Jesus that made them want to follow him. They went back to the boat to explain to Zebedee, their father, where they were going. They knew that he, along with his hired servants, could handle the business very well. After all, Jesus had said he needed them. And something inside said they must answer his call—and follow.

"Come home with Andrew and me for supper," Peter said to Jesus, "and spend the night."

"Thank you, Peter. I would like that." Jesus appreciated the invitation.

"Sabbath will begin at sundown, of course," Peter added, "but there is plenty of food already cooked. John and James, you come, too."

As they reached his cottage, Peter's daughter Rachel met them at the door. "Grandmother is not feeling very well," she said. "I helped her get the Sabbath food cooked, but now she is very tired." Peter's own wife had died a few years before. His mother-in-law Sarah was helping him rear his nine-year-old child.

"Let her rest," said Peter. "We will help you get supper on the table."

The next day was the Sabbath. The fishermen and Jesus went to the synagogue. As they entered, the synagogue leader recognized Jesus.

"Read our scripture for us today," he invited.

Jesus came forward and stood before the congregation. The leader handed him the large scroll. Jesus unrolled it and read from the prophet Isaiah, "The Spirit of the Lord is upon me. He has appointed me to . . .

preach good news to the poor
proclaim freedom to the captives
give sight to the blind
and announce the kingdom of God."

As he sat down, there were murmurs throughout the congregation.

"I've heard about this rabbi, this teacher," whispered one woman to another. "Some say he may be the Messiah, the promised king we have been waiting for."

"He doesn't sound like a king to me," another said. "He sounds more like a servant."

"I heard he read that same passage in the synagogue in Nazareth and they threw him out of town," someone added.

In the congregation there was a man who had been sick for a long time with a disease that had affected his mind. Suddenly he screamed with a loud voice and interrupted the service. Jesus walked over to the man, put his hand on him, and the man became calm.

"Look at that!" exclaimed a woman. "Jesus has healed Absalom. Why, Absalom has been out of his mind for years. Some people say he's had a demon. Now Jesus has healed him!"

Everyone was amazed at what they had seen.

"Jesus read the scripture as though the words applied to *himself.* He not only talks about God, but he is a servant of other people, too," said one man.

When the service was over, Jesus went again to Peter's home. His daughter Rachel ran to them as they turned through the gate.

"Oh, Father," she cried. "Grandmother is very sick. She has a high fever. I have been putting cold towels on her head. Now I can't get her to wake up. I don't know what to do!"

"There, there, Rachel," said Peter as he stooped

down beside her and dried her tears. "We are with you now and we will. . . ."

"Let me go to her," Jesus interrupted.

"Yes, yes, of course," said Peter. And they led him to her.

"Sarah," Jesus said as he gently took her by the hand. She opened her eyes and looked at him. The fever had gone!

"Why am I lying here in bed?" she exclaimed. "I must get up and serve you the food I prepared yesterday before the Sabbath began." She put on her sandals and hurried about her tasks. The family and Jesus enjoyed a fine meal together.

As soon as the sun had set far enough that three stars could be seen in the sky, the Sabbath had ended.

"Jesus!" they suddenly heard voices calling. "Come and heal my crippled son." They looked out the cottage door and saw a crowd of people gathering.

"My mother is blind," he heard another voice say. "Come and give her back her sight."

"My little girl is paralyzed and cannot walk. Come and help her," another said.

Jesus walked into the yard. There were hundreds of people there and in the street. He went through the crowd healing all those who asked. By the light of a full moon he healed, late into the night. None was turned away without getting Jesus' help. Jesus was exhausted as he finally lay down to sleep long after midnight.

Before dawn he was awake again. Silently he left

the house to try to find a quiet place where he could pray. A time alone with God was the way he began every day.

"Master, come," his prayer was interrupted. "Everyone is calling for you." Peter and others had found him.

"I will come," said Jesus. "But I must go to other villages, too. I must preach and teach and heal everywhere, for that is what God wants me to do."

Large crowds now followed him to many places. He would teach from a boat or under a tree. Once he climbed up a hill and the crowd gathered around him. He said to them: "Love your enemies. Do good to those who hate you. . . . Pray for those who mistreat you. . . . If anyone hits you on one cheek, let him strike the other also. . . . Give to everyone who asks."

"Wait, Jesus," someone interrupted. "Can you make all that simpler so we can remember it?"

"All right," said Jesus, "here is a golden rule to go by: Do unto others as you would have them do unto you."

"How should we pray?" a woman asked him.

"Pray like this," Jesus answered. And he taught them what we now call the Lord's Prayer.

A young mother with two small children began to elbow her way through the crowd toward Jesus.

"My children can't see him," she said as he pushed on. "I want my children to see Jesus. I want him to bless them."

"Go back," shouted a disciple. "Jesus is too busy. He doesn't have time for children."

Jesus heard what the disciple had said to the young mother. It made him angry.

"Don't you try to stop the children from coming to me," Jesus commanded. "Let all the children come. The kingdom of God belongs to them."

A young man who was dressed in very fine clothes came to the front of the crowd. He asked, "What must I do to have eternal life?"

"Keep the Ten Commandments," replied Jesus.

"But I have kept the Commandments all my life. What else do I need to do?"

"There is one more thing. Sell all you have and give the money to the poor," Jesus answered.

The young man was sad. He turned and walked away. He was very rich and he did not want to give what he had to the poor.

Jesus was sad, too, as he saw the young man turn and leave. "It is easier for a camel to go through the eye of a needle," he said, "than for a rich person to enter the kingdom."

Some of the people began to snicker. "A camel trying to go through the eye of a needle?" laughed one man. "What a joke. That would be impossible!" Part of what the crowds loved about Jesus was the way he could say something funny to help them understand something important.

The disciples began to get a new understanding of what Jesus had called them to do. They must leave everything behind and follow their Master. This would involve sacrifice. It would mean they would have to give up many things for Jesus. Now there were twelve men who had become disciples and were willing to do this. There were women who were helping Jesus, too.

Peter went back to his home and tried to explain to Sarah and Rachel. "Jesus has called me to follow him. He must go to other parts of Palestine so he can preach and teach and heal. And I must go with him. I hope I can be back soon. Zebedee and his family have said they will help when you need them. Perhaps I can join you later. But now I simply must go."

"Don't worry about us, Father," said Rachel. "Grandmother and I can take care of each other. We are proud that you are a disciple of Jesus. We believe in him, too."

So Peter left everything to follow his Lord.

Chapter 5

Kingdom Stories
about God's People

Daniel worked carefully at his potter's wheel. He had not heard his friend come into his shop there in the village of Magdala.

"Peace, Daniel," Joshua said. "You seem busy today."

"Good morning, Joshua. Yes, I am busy. I have a large order for jars and pitchers. I must get them finished by the end of next week." He continued to shape the soft clay as it spun around on the wheel. "There is to be a wedding in Cana. I am making these jars for the feast."

"Don't let me stop you, but I suppose you already know that Jesus is here in Magdala. People from all around are gathering over beside the lake to hear him. The crowd is even bigger than it was yesterday."

"Don't bother me with such foolishness, Joshua. I have my work to do. I heard Jesus once when he was preaching in Capernaum. I had to laugh when I heard him say, 'Happy are the poor.' The poor are poor because they won't work. They certainly aren't 'happy' or 'blessed.'

"Take me, for instance," continued Daniel, "I work hard. I want to buy things for my family. I don't have time to stop and listen to Jesus. No, Joshua, I must stay at my potter's wheel."

"But it's not just what Jesus says, it is what he *does*," Joshua protested. "He has time for everybody— even people that others think aren't very 'nice' people. You remember Mary of this town who led such a wicked life? There are those here who have even said she had 'seven demons' she was so bad. Our best neighbors didn't want to be seen talking to her. You know the story. Jesus saw her in the crowd and went to her and made her a new person. Now she has left her sinful ways and is one of his followers."

"That won't last," sneered Daniel. "Mary of Magdala—or Mary Magdalene as everybody calls her—will never be any different. You wait and see. Take Ahab, the tax collector, for example. He decided to become a follower of Jesus. That lasted about a week. Now he is back to his old ways.

"I've heard Jesus once. Some won't even take the time to do that," Daniel concluded.

Joshua left the shop. *It is sad*, he thought to himself, shaking his head. *Very sad. I wish Daniel could understand. People respond to Jesus in such different ways.*

Just then he felt something tugging at his robe. He looked down. Two children were beside him.

"Good morning, Esther. Good morning, Sol-

omon. Peace to you." Joshua greeted his niece and nephew.

"Jesus is in town today," exclaimed Esther. "We want to go hear him. Please take us to hear him, Uncle Joshua. Mother said we couldn't go by ourselves."

"We want to hear Jesus tell some stories," added her younger brother.

"Yes, of course. I will take you. I was planning to go there myself anyway."

They found a crowd of people sitting on the shore by the sea. Children of all ages, old people, and young people were listening as Jesus talked to them from the boat in which he was sitting. Joshua noticed Mary Magdalene sitting with the disciples close to the boat.

"Listen," they heard him say, "see that farmer sowing seed over there?" The people turned and looked. "As he sows his seed, some falls on the path and won't grow at all. Some of it falls on rocky ground that is covered only with a thin layer of dirt. That seed will grow quickly, but it soon dies because the roots can't go very deep."

Every eye was on the farmer as Jesus spoke. "Some of that seed is falling in a patch of thorny weeds. It may grow a little, but the weeds will finally choke it out.

"But," said Jesus, "some of the seed is falling on good soil. It will grow and produce a large crop of

wheat. This," said Jesus, "is a story about the kingdom of God."

"What does he mean, Uncle Joshua?" asked Solomon. "I don't understand."

Joshua began to remember the conversation he
had had earlier that morning in the potter's shop.

"Sowing seed is like telling people about the
kingdom of God," Joshua explained. "Some people
won't listen at all to the message of the kingdom.
That would be like the seed that fell on the path. It
would never grow.

"Other people hear and believe for a little while

and then go back to their old ways." Joshua thought of Ahab, the tax collector, and how he had done just that.

"For some, other things choke out the message of the kingdom," he said, thinking of the way Daniel was letting his desire for money come first.

"But some people, Solomon, are like the good soil. They hear the message and really believe and follow Jesus." Joshua was thinking especially of Mary Magdalene and of Peter, Andrew, John, and others who were followers and disciples of Jesus.

Someone in the crowd said, "Jesus, what do you mean by the kingdom? I don't see it anywhere."

Jesus got out of the boat and walked over to the field. He found a tiny seed. He held it up and said, "Do you see this seed?"

"No, it's too little. I can't see it," answered the man who had asked the question.

"The kingdom of God is like this seed," said Jesus. "You can't see it, but when it grows it becomes as big as a tree and even the birds can make nests in its branches. The kingdom of God begins small, but grows and grows within you."

A woman was in the crowd who had with her a basket of bread. Jesus picked up one of her loaves and said, "The kingdom is like this bread. It took yeast to make the bread rise. You can't see yeast at work, but you can all see what it *does*. It makes flour become a delicious loaf of bread."

The people began to understand more about the

kingdom as Jesus taught them in parables, or stories.

A lawyer in the crowd, however, challenged Jesus. "You talk about the kingdom, Jesus. Kingdoms have to have laws. What is the greatest law in this kingdom you talk about?"

"You are a lawyer. You know what that law is," Jesus replied. "Love the Lord with all your heart, mind, and soul, and your neighbor as yourself."

"But who is my neighbor?" the lawyer asked. Jesus then told another story:

As a traveler turned a bend on the road from Jerusalem to Jericho, three robbers armed with heavy wooden clubs jumped from behind a large boulder.

"Give us your money!" one shouted.

"No," the traveler said as he clutched his purse close to his side. "I'll need my money when I get to Jericho. Don't take my money!"

"We need it more than you do," sneered another robber as he hit him on the back with a club. The traveler turned to try to defend himself just as the third robber struck him over the head. The blow knocked him unconscious. He fell to the ground.

"Let's take his coat, too," said a robber, laughing. "He'll never need it again."

The robbers took everything the man had. Then they left him lying in the desert to die.

Gradually, though, the poor traveler regained consciousness, although he still could not move or speak.

"Someone is coming," he thought. "Maybe I can get help."

The traveler saw that it was a priest—all dressed in his robe, ready to conduct services at the Temple. But the priest did not stay. He passed by on the opposite side of the road.

In a little while someone else came by. This, too, was a religious leader—a Levite. But he, too, passed on by.

The injured man had almost given up hope when a Samaritan came by. As you know, our people have hated the Samaritans for many years. When I was a boy I remember that my family would travel miles out of the way to avoid going through Samaria.

But this Samaritan was filled with pity. Even though the injured man was from a different culture, he stopped to help. He cleaned the man's wounds and bandaged them. He gently put the injured man on his own donkey and took him to an inn.

"Take care of my friend," the Samaritan told the innkeeper as he handed him silver coins. "If I owe more, I will pay you when I come again."

"Now," said Jesus to the lawyer, "which of these three was a neighbor to the man who was hurt?"

"The one who was kind to him, of course."

"You go and do likewise. Loving God and loving your neighbor as yourself are the most important 'laws' of God's kingdom."

"Uncle Joshua," said Esther with excitement, "I think I understand what Jesus means. The way we show that we are really God's people—a part of God's kingdom—is the way we treat others."

"Yes, Esther, I think you are like the good soil in Jesus' first parable. You are beginning to understand. In your heart the seed will grow."

Chapter 6

The Gift of a Boy

"Have you seen Benjamin?" Naomi asked Tabitha at the village well in Bethsaida. "My son left home early this morning to go over by the lake to hear Jesus. I packed him a lunch, but I had no idea he would be gone so long. It is almost sunset and he hasn't come home."

"No, I haven't seen him," replied Tabitha. "But don't worry, Naomi. There are other people from the town who have gone to hear Jesus. Benjamin will be all right."

Naomi made her way from shop to shop—always with the same question, "Have you seen Benjamin?" She stopped at the stall where leather goods were sold. Nathan the shopkeeper was seated surrounded by sandals and knapsacks. He was dressed in a robe with a long fringe and tassles that all good Pharisees wore. Strapped to his forehead was a little box with a verse of scripture in it.

"Have you seen Benjamin?" asked Naomi. "My boy went to hear Jesus early this morning and he hasn't come home. I thought maybe he and the other boys had come by here."

"So your boy went to hear Jesus! I've heard him. I followed the crowd yesterday to the place where he was preaching. The man is a fake. He can't be from God. I wouldn't let any child of mine go hear him. That traveling teacher is doing all kinds of things against our religion. Why, he even breaks the Ten Commandments. 'Remember the sabbath day to keep it holy' it says in the law of Moses. That means absolutely no work on that holy day. But Jesus let his disciples pluck grain from the wheat field when they were hungry on the Sabbath. That was breaking the Sabbath law. Gathering grain is work, you know. He can't be a man of God if he breaks the law of Moses. But I am sorry Benjamin seems to be lost. If he stops by my shop I will send him home. He ought to be punished for being out so late." Nathan had a stern view about rearing children.

As Naomi left the leather shop, she saw Isaac the basketmaker coming into town, his donkey piled high with baskets to sell.

"Isaac," she called, "Isaac." She ran to talk with him. "Have you seen Benjamin?" she asked her same question once again. "He went to hear Jesus early this morning and he has not come home. I thought you might have seen him as you came down the road into town."

"No, Naomi, I did not see Benjamin on the road. He went to see Jesus, you say?" Isaac looked both ways to be sure no one was listening. He leaned toward her and whispered, "We want to make Jesus king in Israel, you know. The other Zealots and I are ready to fight to help him overthrow Rome. Jesus preaches the kingdom of God. We know this means revolution. We will cut the throats of every Roman in the land—and make Jesus our king." Isaac fingered the dagger he and other Zealots always wore beneath their robes.

"So Benjamin has gone to hear Jesus, has he?" Naomi was startled by the voice behind her. In spite of their whispered conversation, they had been overheard. Eli, a Sadducee and a member of the town council, had silently joined them. "Isaac, you want Jesus to lead a revolt against Rome, but that would be a mistake. It would make our situation much worse than it is. Leave well enough alone, that is what I say. You have to know how to get along with these Romans. Some of us have learned to play their game. There are some compromises we have to make, of course, but it is for a good cause. This Jesus you were talking about is making all kinds of trouble for us. Personally, I think he ought to be arrested along with all his followers. I was talking with some of the other Sadducees who are on the Sanhedrin, and they agree with me. We can't let Jesus continue. We must put a stop to what he is doing."

Naomi now had a new fear. Perhaps her son had been arrested for even going to hear Jesus!

Twilight had come. The village square was

becoming deserted as people returned to their homes for the night. Only a few of the shops were still open. Naomi kept her watch. She looked down the narrow streets again and again hoping to see Benjamin.

"Mother, Mother," she heard his voice. He had seen her and was calling to her as he ran. "Guess what happened!"

"Benjamin! Where in the world have you been? I told you not to stay long. Why didn't you come home sooner?" Naomi was furious with him. "I told you. . . ."

"But Mother, I couldn't. It was just wonderful. I want to tell you all about it. Late this afternoon. . . ."

"No excuses, young man. You should have been home long ago. I told you before you left that you were not to stay all day."

By this time others from the town who had been to hear Jesus had joined Benjamin and his mother at the well. They had walked home more slowly than the boy.

"Please let the boy tell you his story." It was Andrew, one of Jesus' disciples who also lived in Bethsaida, who spoke. "He really does have a story that you must hear." Andrew put his hand on the boy's shoulder.

"Oh, Mother, it has been the most wonderful day. There were thousands and thousands of people out there to hear Jesus. He healed people—and one of them was old Jesse, the blind man that lives right

here in Bethsaida. I saw him heal a little crippled girl and a boy who was an epileptic. He told us stories about the kingdom of God. Children crowded all around him and he held them in his lap and patted them on the heads and loved them. It began to get late and everybody was hungry. But there in the grassy field there was no food—except my lunch."

"Benjamin offered his lunch," interrupted Andrew. "I took him and his lunch to Jesus. I didn't see how that little lunch of five loaves and two fishes would do much good. It certainly couldn't feed all those people, but it was all we had."

"Jesus said a prayer," added Benjamin. "He asked God to bless my lunch. Then the disciples began to pass food to the crowd. And would you believe it? My lunch had become enough to feed all those five thousand people. It was a miracle, Mother. I don't know how it happened; it was a miracle."

"Yes, everybody was fed. No one had to go away hungry. And there was enough food left over to fill twelve baskets!" Andrew told Naomi.

The crowd that had returned from the countryside had been joined by the shopkeepers and others as the marketplace closed for the night. They were all amazed at what they heard. There was a variety of responses from the townspeople.

Now is surely the time, mused Isaac, the Zealot, to himself. *With all that public support, this is the time to get rid of the Romans. We will overthrow Rome. Jesus will lead us into battle—and we will crown him our king.*

Eli, the Sadducee, had other thoughts. *Jesus is going to get himself killed and some of the rest of us with him if he isn't careful. We must put a stop to what he is doing.*

Nathan, the Pharisee, could not help thinking about his religion and how Jesus was leading people away from the law of Moses. He had heard Jesus say, "I have come not to *destroy* the law but to *fulfill* it." But it surely seemed to him that Jesus was trying to destroy *everything.* He didn't like it one bit. *Our Jewish laws must be upheld,* he said to himself.

Those who had been healed by Jesus had different thoughts. The little girl who had been crippled ran and skipped as she thought of what Jesus had done for her. Old Jesse, the blind man whom Jesus

had healed, said over and over again, "I was blind, but now I can see."

Naomi had found her boy at last. She was confused by what he and others were saying. "Come on home to bed, son," she said. "It is late. You can tell me more about the day's adventures in the morning." With her arm around him, they walked together toward their cottage.

"What a day this has been!" said Benjamin. "I don't understand what happened. All I know is that Jesus took what I brought him and fed five thousand people. I saw him healing the sick, feeding the hungry, telling us stories, and loving us all. I had a part. Jesus used what I brought to him to help other people. Maybe that is something of what the kingdom of God is all about."

Chapter 7

We Welcome Our King

"Hey, there. Why are you untying our donkey?" Rebecca yelled at the strangers. She stopped playing hopscotch and ran toward the house. "Father, two men are stealing our colt."

Samuel followed Rebecca into the yard. "I think I know what must be happening." He patted her on the head. "Don't worry, Rebecca." He greeted the two men at the gate. "Why are you untying our donkey?" Samuel repeated.

"The Master needs it," said Peter. He and John had been told by Jesus exactly what they were to say—a kind of prearranged password.

"Ah, yes, my friends. Take the donkey. I have been expecting you."

"What was that all about?" asked Rebecca.

"Jesus and I arranged this several days ago. I understand that he plans to ride our donkey into Jerusalem later today. I am planning to go into the city myself. I have an idea this may be the time that our Master will declare that he is the new king in

Israel. He will show the people that he is the Messiah."

"Oh, may I go with you, Father? Please let me go." Rebecca jumped with excitement.

"Of course, you may. And your sister Ruth, too. All of Jesus' followers will be there. Jerusalem will be crowded with people. This is Passover season, you know, and thousands have come for the feast. When we celebrate the deliverance of God's people, it is a special time."

Samuel and his daughters joined the throng. He could sense the excitement of the crowd as he and his daughters pushed along to reach the Temple area in Jerusalem. He overheard what people were saying along the way.

"I am sure Jesus must be the promised Messiah," one man said. Then he asked, "What do you suppose he will do today when he rides into town?" Another said, "I have seen him heal the blind and the crippled. Probably he will heal all the people in Jerusalem. Then everybody will know he is the Messiah."

"I was with Jesus when he fed five thousand people with only five loaves and two fish," said a young mother to a friend who stood beside her. "It was a miracle! I thought we should crown him king that day, but perhaps he wanted us to wait until today. He'll do an even greater miracle here in the capital city. You watch and see. Do you think we should crown him at the Temple—or should we do it at the governor's Judgment Hall?"

Samuel heard another man say, "Jesus is a prophet. I believe he will go right to the Temple. When the religious leaders hear him, they, too, will believe."

Another said, "He held my little child in his arms. The Master's words were, 'Except you become as a little child, you cannot enter the kingdom.' Jesus preaches the kingdom of God, you know. This is the day for us to crown him king."

As the crowd milled around Samuel and his girls, he knew this must be the time for something really significant to happen. Everybody seemed ready to follow Jesus.

As they waited they began to hear shouting and singing. Samuel lifted Ruth to his shoulders so she could see above the crowd.

"I see him, Father!" Ruth shouted. "Jesus is coming! He is riding on our donkey!"

Children threw flowers in his path. Some people threw their coats in the road for Jesus to ride across. Others cut palm branches and waved them as he passed. Children and adults together sang: "Hosanna, hosanna. Save us. Praise to the Son of David. God bless the king who comes in the name of the Lord."

Rebecca and Ruth each waved a palm branch and raised their voices in songs of praise.

Isaac the Zealot was in the crowd. "Hail, King Jesus," he called. "Give the word and we will take up our swords and kill the Romans for you. Barabbas was our leader but he has been arrested. You can take his

place. Be our leader and we will put you on the throne. Then all God's people will be free."

Jesus looked at Isaac with sadness. "No, Isaac," replied Jesus. "The kingdom of God is within you. Love your enemies. Do good to those who persecute you. That's the way to be the people of God."

Samuel wondered as he heard those words.

Maybe Jesus would somehow be a different kind of king from what they all expected. He had not ridden into the capital city of Jerusalem on a horse or in a war chariot as a king preparing for battle would have done. But he rode on a *donkey*. He recalled the words of the prophet Zechariah who had said: "Shout

71

for joy, your king is coming to you. He comes triumphant and victorious riding on a *donkey*. . . . Your king will make peace among the nations. He will rule the world."

The crowd got larger and larger as Jesus rode into the city. "Hosanna. Praise the Son of David," children along the way continued to sing.

Not all the people were singing praises, however. Some were angry at what they saw happening.

Nathan, the Pharisee, elbowed his way through the crowd until he was right beside Jesus. "Make these children stop this singing. You are no king. Make the children be quiet."

"I tell you, Nathan, they speak the truth." said Jesus. "If the children did not sing, the stones themselves would begin to shout."

Jesus rode to the Temple. He got off the donkey and carefully tied it to a tree.

Samuel and his girls followed him. In the Temple, they saw Jesus stand very still as he looked around. Before him were merchants who sold animals and birds to those who came to the Temple to make sacrifices. Money changers sat behind their tables counting coins.

Suddenly the mood changed. Instead of the quiet man of peace they had seen before, they saw Jesus become furious! He began to drive the cattle and sheep out of the Temple. He opened the cages of the pigeons and feathers flew. Coins clanked to the floor as Jesus upset tables.

"My father's house is to be a house of prayer, but you have made it a den of thieves! Religious ceremonies are not a chance for people to become rich!" Jesus was shouting with anger in his voice.

The religious leaders were now angry, too. Priests, Pharisees, scribes, Sadducees saw Jesus upsetting everything.

"We must stop this man," Nathan the Pharisee exploded. "Something must be done!"

"People seem ready to crown him king," another Pharisee growled.

"Yes, this has gone too far. It was bad enough for Jesus, that teacher from Nazareth, to ride into Jerusalem with everyone singing his praises. But now this!" a Sadducee exclaimed.

"Right here in the Temple, creating such a scene. It's inexcusable!" The religious leaders were all talking at once.

Caiaphas, the high priest, rose and raised his hand in a call for silence.

"There is only one thing that can be done," the high priest said, stroking his beard. "Come closer, men." As the leaders gathered around him, he whispered, "Yes, there is only one way. We must have Jesus killed."

Samuel was stunned and frightened at what he had overheard. He was glad that his daughters had been playing with a small lamb and had not heard the whispered conversation of the religious leaders.

He called his children and quickly left the Temple. As they walked toward Bethany, Ruth said, "Isn't it wonderful the way everyone loves Jesus?"

"Yes," agreed Rebecca. "I'll bet he will be crowned king before the week is over."

Samuel did not know how to reply. *I wonder,* he thought. *I wonder what is going to happen.*

Chapter 8

The
Trial of Our King

The night was as silent as it was black. The only sound the disciples could hear was the voice of Jesus as he prayed.

Their Master had gone to a lonely spot on the Mount of Olives to pray. The disciples knew that Jesus was troubled. They could see only his faint outline through the darkness. Jesus had thrown himself on the ground as he struggled in prayer.

They heard the sobs as Jesus prayed, "Father, if it is possible, let there be some other way. I don't want to go through all the suffering that is before me." Sweat rolled down his forehead. His voice choked with tears as he said, "And yet, my Father, I will do your will. It is not my own will but yours that must be done." He wiped his face on the sleeve of his robe.

Suddenly the dark and peaceful garden was filled with light and confusion. Soldiers and religious leaders made their way up the hillside. Torches and lanterns lighted their way. They were marching toward Jesus.

The mood was very different from the one four

days earlier. On the Sabbath before, Jesus had ridden triumphantly into Jerusalem on a small donkey. Many had hailed him a king. But now, instead of palm branches, people waved clubs and swords. The temple guards and religious leaders were led by Judas, one of Jesus' own disciples.

"Hello there, Master," said Judas as he kissed him on the cheek.

"Arrest that man," shouted one of the guards. "The one Judas kissed is Jesus. That is the sign he told us he would use."

Armed guards ran to seize Jesus. Jesus walked calmly toward his captors. "I'm the one you want. Let the others go."

Peter pulled a dagger from his belt and lashed out at one of the guards.

"Put your weapon away, Peter," said Jesus. "My kingdom is not one of violence, but of love and peace."

A guard tied Jesus' hands together. Confused and frightened, most of the disciples ran from the garden. Only Peter lingered behind, hiding now in the shadows. When he was sure he wouldn't be noticed, he followed as the soldiers led his Master away.

The Jerusalem streets were dark except for the light from the soldiers' torches. Peter crept silently some distance behind. As he followed, he kept thinking of all the events that had taken place earlier that evening.

He recalled the Passover meal of roast lamb and unleavened bread that the disciples had eaten with Jesus in the upper room. Peter had been full of hope then. *Perhaps the kingdom is about to come,* he had thought.

He remembered, however, that Jesus had acted not like a king, but like a servant. He had washed all the disciples' feet.

Peter remembered that Jesus had talked not about conquering Rome, but about dying. He had said that one of the disciples would actually betray him. *Now we know whom he meant,* Peter thought. *And to think that Judas betrayed our master with a kiss!*

But Peter also remembered that Jesus had said that even he, Peter, would deny he ever knew him.

I'll never let you down, Peter recalled promising Jesus. *You can count on me.*

And then Jesus had said, "Peter, before the rooster crows tomorrow morning, you will have denied me three times."

Peter was jolted from his memories when he arrived at the courtyard of Caiaphas, the high priest. He realized the religious council was already meeting. Jesus was being questioned by the Sanhedrin inside the house. The elders, scribes, Pharisees, and Sadducees listened while people made false charges against Jesus as they testified at the trial.

Peter remained in the shadows in the courtyard. Roman soldiers and the Temple guards who had arrested Jesus hovered around a fire. The night air was cold.

Tamar, a young servant girl of the high priest, threw fresh wood on the fire. By its light she caught a glimpse of Peter moving closer to the warmth of the flames.

"Say," she said, "you are one of Jesus' disciples."

"You are mistaken," replied Peter, frightened that the guards might arrest him, too. "I never saw that prisoner before."

Peter moved further back into the shadows. Another servant girl saw him as she brought wine to the guards. She said to those around her, "He is one of the disciples. I've seen him before with Jesus."

"Don't accuse me of being the friend of a common criminal!" Peter swore. "I do not know that man!"

"Come now," one of the guards laughed. "I can tell by the way you talk. You are from Galilee as is this Jesus. Your accent gives you away. I am sure you are one of his disciples."

With that, Peter became angry. "I told you I don't know the prisoner. I never saw him before."

As Peter said those words, Jesus was being led through the courtyard. He looked at Peter. In the distance a rooster crowed. Peter remembered the words Jesus had spoken to him earlier that evening, "Before the rooster crows tomorrow morning, three times you will have denied you ever knew me."

Peter turned and ran from the courtyard. At a safe distance, he threw himself down beside the road and cried. He pounded the ground and sobbed.

"What have I done?" he cried. "I have denied my Lord! How can I ever be forgiven?"

Back at the fire, the two servant girls were giggling. "What a coward that man is," laughed Tamar. "Just because we recognized him as a disciple, he cursed and swore."

At dawn, the religious council declared, "Jesus must die. Any man who claims to be the Messiah— King of the Jews—must be put to death."

"Take him to Pontius Pilate," Caiaphas shouted to the guards. "The Roman governor must pronounce the sentence of death and Roman soldiers must carry out the execution."

The guards obeyed the order and led Jesus away to Pilate's Judgment Hall.

Even though it was barely daylight, a crowd was gathering on the street. Many filed through the gate to the courtyard of the Judgment Hall to watch the trial. Even some of Jesus' friends had heard what was happening to their master and crept inside the gate.

"This man has broken our law. He claims to be the Messiah—King of the Jews," Caiaphas shouted to the Roman governor. "According to our law he must die. But we religious leaders cannot pronounce the death sentence. Only Rome can do that. We know that you, O mighty governor, would want no king but Caesar. You will agree that this Jesus should die!"

"Are you a king?" Pilate asked as he pointed his finger at Jesus.

"I am a king, but my kingdom is not of this world. It is a kingdom of love and peace."

Pilate knew Jesus was not guilty. "This man is innocent," he said to the high priest. "As you know," he continued, "at Passover season I always set a prisoner free. This year I will release Jesus. Yes, since Jesus of Nazareth has committed no crime, I will let him go free!"

Jesus' friends who were watching the trial were thrilled when they heard those words. Jesus was going to be set free! He would not be crucified after all! This news was too good to keep. They must find the disciples and tell them the news. As fast as they could, they ran to the upper room, hoping to find some of the disciples.

But the friends had left the trial too soon. "No!" shouted the angry mob. "Crucify Jesus! Release Barabbas!"

"Barabbas tried to lead a revolt against Rome. He is a Zealot," one man shouted. "Let him go free — even though he is a murderer and a rebel."

The voices of the mob grew louder and louder as they called for the death sentence for Jesus. "Crucify him, crucify him," they screamed.

"I will have the prisoner whipped and then released. That should satisfy you. For I find this Jesus — your 'king' — is an innocent man."

"Centurion," Pilate called to a Roman officer. "Take the prisoner and beat him."

The soldiers chained Jesus to a post. With heavy leather straps, they struck him blow after blow on his bare back. They put a purple robe on him and thrust a crown of thorns on his head. "Hail, King of the Jews," the soldiers laughed as they led him back to Pilate.

"I find no crime in this man," Pilate said once more. "I now release him. He is a free man."

"No, never," the mob shouted. "Crucify Jesus! Release Barabbas!"

"But Jesus is your 'king'," mocked Pilate. "Do you want me to crucify your king?"

"We have no king but the Emperor of Rome," said the high priest. "Crucify Jesus. Release Barabbas."

Reluctantly, Pilate gave in to their demands.

"As you wish," said the governor. Even Pilate was no match for the religious leaders. "As you wish."

Meanwhile, the friends who had watched the trial found the disciples in the upper room.

The Trial of Our King

"We have just come from Pilate's Judgment Hall," panted one of the friends as he tried to catch his breath. "Pilate is going to set Jesus free! We heard him say so."

"You know the custom," the other friend interrupted. "Every year at Passover time a prisoner is released. This year the governor said he would release Jesus. 'Jesus is an innocent man,' I heard Pilate say," the friend continued. "Jesus is going to be set free. He probably will be coming here to the upper room any minute."

"I knew Jesus wouldn't really be killed," the disciple Matthew said. "All that talk about dying he did tonight at supper. I *knew* he would be all right."

The friends waited in the upper room with the disciples as the minutes dragged by. Jesus did not come.

"I will go back to the Judgment Hall to see what happened," one of the friends offered. "The Master should be here by now. I will come back and bring you news."

As the friend approached the gate he could hear the shouts of the angry mob. "Release the prisoner," the friend heard Pilate command in a loud voice. "The other man will be crucified."

The friend stood still in his tracks. "I will wait here, outside the gate," he said to himself. "I can be the one to take Jesus with me to the upper room. I told the disciples I would bring them news. I will do even better than that. I will take them our Master instead."

In the early light of dawn the freed prisoner walked through the gate. His head was held high in triumph. But the friend saw that the prisoner who had been given his freedom was not Jesus. It was Barabbas!

"I am free! I am a free man!" the rebel shouted. "Jesus is to die on the cross in my place."

Far away in the distance Jesus was being led toward Calvary, the place where he would be crucified.

Chapter 9

God So Loved

"**M**ove, prisoner," growled the soldier in charge. "The cross you carry can't be *that* heavy." With a whip, he gave Jesus a sharp lash across his back. Jesus fell to his knees from the impact. On his head he wore a crown of thorns. Soldiers had harshly thrust it on him as they had mocked him as a king. Jesus, along with two thieves, was in a procession that moved through the streets of Jerusalem. He and the other prisoners were on their way to be crucified. They each were forced to carry the heavy wooden crossbar to which they would be nailed.

A small group of women who loved Jesus followed along in the procession going to Calvary, outside the city wall, where the crucifixion would take place. One of them rushed to him. She wiped his bloodstained face with a towel. Another gave him a sip of water from a small water jar she carried. Jesus tried to smile in gratitude.

The streets of Jerusalem were filled with people on that bright spring Friday. From many places men, women, and children had come to Jerusalem to celebrate Passover in remembrance of the deliverance of God's people from slavery in the days of Moses. Many of them were unconcerned as the procession passed. Others enjoyed watching the cruel treatment the condemned men were getting. "Messiah, are you? King of the Jews! What a joke!" a man on the street laughed. A woman threw a handful of rotten fruit into Jesus' face.

Four soldiers formed a square around each prisoner. Another soldier carried a large sign in front of each one telling what crime the condemned man had committed. The soldiers led the prisoners on the longest possible route through the city. Rome wanted people to see what happened to those who dared to break the laws of Rome. The sign being carried in front of Jesus said, "Jesus of Nazareth, King of the Jews."

The procession to Calvary was about to end. The women knew Jesus and the two thieves would soon be nailed to their crosses.

Salome, Mary Magdalene, and the others would not watch as the nails were driven into Jesus' wrists. They covered their eyes, but they heard the hammering. They heard the coarse laughter of the soldiers and the mocking of the crowd. When they opened their eyes, they saw Jesus on the center cross. And the sign that was carried before him in the procession had been nailed above his head.

John, one of Jesus' disciples, joined the women. He brought with him Jesus' mother, Mary. Her frail body was stooped in grief. Her face was veiled. John had his arm lovingly around her. He was the only one of Jesus' disciples who had had the courage to come to the cross. The others had fled and were hiding. They were afraid they, too, might be arrested and killed. In the small group of which John and Mary became a part, few words were spoken. Each person just sobbed and wept. Their grief was hard to bear.

Around the cross were Roman soldiers who amused themselves with games of chance. Some of the religious leaders who had helped arrange Jesus' arrest were there. Others came just to watch. Executions always attracted large crowds. This one was no exception. The people in the crowd laughed and joked. Men, women, and even some children had come to see the event.

As Jesus' followers stood silently in their sorrow, they heard their Master's voice ring out loud and clear. "Father, forgive them, for they do not know what they are doing."

"How can that be?" Salome broke the silence. "How can Jesus ask God to forgive those cruel people who have nailed him to a cross? 'Forgive them.' He asks God to forgive them!"

"That is the kind of life he lived," Joanna quietly replied. "His God, *our* God, is one who *forgives*. Even in his dying hours, Jesus is showing what God is really like."

The crowd had grown larger around the cross.

"Come down from the cross, if you are the Son of

God," one of the spectators taunted. "Some king you are. You can't even save yourself." The hillside rang with the mocking laughter of the soldiers and the crowd.

Though it was noon, the sky was getting dark. Heavy clouds began to blot out the sun. Frightened by the strange darkness, the crowd became silent. Almost the only sounds now were the sobs of the women followers who wept nearby.

Time dragged on. Jesus was growing weaker. "I'm thirsty." His parched throat could hardly say the words.

Made anxious by the threatening sky, many who had come to scoff went home. Only the faithful followers, the soldiers, and a few others remained. Suddenly the earth began to tremble.

"It's an earthquake!" screamed Salome. "We are having an earthquake!" The tremor stopped as quickly as it had come.

They heard Jesus' voice once again. He was sobbing as he cried, "My God, my God, why have you forsaken me?"

The women could not believe what they heard. Their master, whose faith had been so strong, now felt completely deserted—even by God!

Only Mary, Jesus' mother, spoke. "I must go to him. John, take me to him. I am his mother and I must go nearer to the cross."

John gently led her closer to the cross. Jesus lifted his head as he saw his mother and John stand-

ing near him. He spoke in a hoarse voice. "Mother . . . your son." He tried to nod toward John. Then, "John . . . your mother." Mary and John knew what he meant. She put her head on John's shoulder and cried. John sheltered her in his arms. He knew that from that time on he would care for her as though she were his own mother.

They heard Jesus' voice again. It was strong once more. He gave what sounded like a cry of victory. "It is finished." And then they heard him whisper, "Father, into your hands I commit my spirit." He threw his thorn-crowned head back in one last jerk of pain. Then it fell peacefully forward. Jesus had breathed his last.

As Mary heard Jesus' last words, she remembered hearing him say them many times before when he was a child. They were part of a psalm that he and other children often said before going to sleep each night. She knew Jesus had died as though in the arms of a loving parent.

John looked up at the face of Jesus, and once more at the sign at the top of the cross. *Jesus of Nazareth, King of the Jews*. The sign was written in three languages—Latin, Greek, and Hebrew. It was written so all could read it. *A king*, thought John. *A king for all people. But the kingdom he talked about never came*. He shook his head. *Our king is dead*.

But John had other thoughts, too, as he stood looking up into the face of Jesus. He remembered the words John the Baptizer had used about Jesus the day he was baptized. "Behold the Lamb of God who takes away the sins of the world," the Baptizer had said. These words reminded John of the sacrificial lamb that was always a part of Passover. *Do you suppose?* John said to himself. He wondered.

Two men whom Mary and John did not know joined them at the foot of the cross. The four stood in silence for a while, with heads bowed in reverence. Finally one of the strangers broke the silence.

"I am Joseph from the town of Arimathea," said one of the men in a quiet voice. "My friend and I have come to help with the burial of Jesus. I have a cave tomb in a nearby garden where we can place his body."

The other man remained quiet. But finally he spoke softly.

"My name is Nicodemus. I was a secret follower of Jesus. I am a Pharisee—one of the religious leaders. I am ashamed to say I was afraid to follow Jesus openly. I came to him only at night so that no one would know."

Nicodemus paused. He lifted his head and looked into the face of the man on the cross.

"I remember something Jesus once said to me. 'For God so loved the world that he gave his son . . . .' Now I think I understand."

Chapter 10

The First Easter

Twilight had come at last, and the Sabbath was over. Mary Magdalene, Salome, and Joanna made their way down the narrow Jerusalem street.

"I hope we can find Cyrus, the Persian merchant," Salome said. "His stall is probably open. He has the finest selection of perfumes. Don't you think we ought to get some of those spices that come from Egypt?" Salome seemed to find comfort in talking. The other women walked along beside her, their silence broken only by an occasional sigh or sob.

It had been such a long Sabbath. Before it began on Friday evening they had watched as Jesus' body was placed in a cave tomb in a garden. There had been no time for a proper burial then. Jesus had died on the cross at 3:00 and the Sabbath began at 6:00 as the sun set.

Joseph of Arimathea and Nicodemus had gently taken the Savior from the cross. They had carried the body to Joseph's garden tomb and reverently wrapped it in grave clothes. They had placed the body on a shelf inside the cave and, with the help of some other strong men, had rolled a large stone to close the entrance. The women had watched the hasty burial as they wept and sobbed. On Friday there had been no time to prepare the body for burial as was the custom. They had to wait. But the moment the Sabbath ended the women were on their way to the shops to purchase the necessary spices.

"How could this have happened?" Salome continued. "How could our Master have ended such a failure? I thought he was the Messiah and would establish his kingdom now, here in Jerusalem. I wanted my sons to have top places in the new order. I remember the day so well three years ago when Jesus called my sons, James and John, to be his disciples. The boys and their father were fishing just off the shore of Lake Galilee. The Master talked with the boys, and they decided right then and there to follow him. They left my husband and the hired servants in the boat and became his disciples. I've followed Jesus, too, especially since Zebedee died. I've washed clothes, cooked, and done what I could. I probably shouldn't say it, but Jesus could never have reached so many people if we women had not given our support. Why has it all ended like this?"

The other women continued their silence. Joanna, the wife of Chuza who worked in Herod's court, was wealthy, too. *Poor Salome,* she thought, *still bragging about how much she did for Jesus! We all did all we could and look what it's come to.* Mary Magdalene was also wondering why Jesus had to die. She had had no money to give, but she had given her love and devotion. She was thinking not of what she had done for Jesus, but of what he had done for her. Mary remembered that Jesus had healed her and made her a new person. He had given her a new kind of life. The women walked in silence as they, too, remembered and tried to understand what this all meant.

They reached the shop of Cyrus, found it open, and made their purchases. Then, in the gathering darkness, they made their way back to the Jerusalem home where they were guests and would spend the night.

None of the women slept very much that night, however. They wanted to be at Jesus' grave at the first glimmer of light. As the Roman bugle sounded "cock-crow" across the city, they arose and prepared to start to the tomb.

As the women left the cottage, Mary Magdalene carried a lamp to light their way. Only faint wisps of gray began to brighten the eastern sky. They walked faster and faster as they passed through the sleeping city. Each clutched close to her robe a jar of precious spice to anoint the body of Jesus.

These three were joined by other women along the way who also wanted to visit Jesus' tomb. Suddenly the earth began to tremble.

"What was that?" cried Mary, stopping in her tracks. "It felt like an earthquake!" The others hovered close beside her.

"There was another earthquake Friday afternoon.

Remember?" Joanna whispered. "The whole world seems to be crumbling."

And indeed it was.

Their world *had* crumbled. They had believed Jesus of Nazareth to be the promised Messiah! How could his ministry have ended in such defeat? And such humiliating defeat! Their Master had been executed like a common criminal—crucified between two thieves!

The earth tremor stopped. They resumed walking to the tomb. Their pace quickened. The sky was turning from pink to gold. They no longer needed the lamplight, so Mary blew it out. Instead of walking, now the women began to run through the city gate and up the hill toward the tomb.

"Look!" shouted Mary Magdalene, stopping suddenly. "The stone has been rolled away. Someone must have stolen our Lord's body. As if killing him were not enough, they have now taken his body and hidden it from us." Mary was angry.

The other women, however, were afraid. Who could have done this final injustice to their Lord? On Friday, they had seen the heavy stone rolled to the entrance to the cave tomb. They knew armed guards had been assigned to watch the tomb to keep anyone from stealing the body. But in spite of all that the stone had been rolled away and the tomb was apparently empty. They trembled in fright—just as the earth had trembled a few minutes before.

In fear the women ran back to the city to find the disciples. They must tell them what had happened. They found the eleven men, sitting silently, their hopes shattered, in the upper room where they had eaten the last supper with Jesus.

"We have just come from Jesus' tomb," said Salome breathlessly, as she and the other women dashed into the room. Her yellow robe was wet with perspiration. "As soon as we got into the garden, we could see that the stone had been rolled away. That great heavy stone was moved to one side of the opening to the cave. . . ."

"First we thought someone had stolen our Lord's body as a kind of cruel joke," Mary Magdalene interrupted, her voice trembling as she spoke. "We moved closer to the tomb. . . ."

"Then a young man spoke to us," Joanna added, "and said Jesus had risen from the dead."

"Not one man," corrected Salome. "I saw two men. 'Why do you seek the living among the dead?' they asked us."

"It seemed to me they were angels who spoke to us," one of the others said. Everyone seemed to be talking at once.

"Calm down," said Thomas. "Don't be so excited. You are just imagining things. We know how upset you are, but. . . ."

"We aren't imagining anything," Salome interrupted. "The stone *was* rolled away. The angels said,

'He is not here. He is risen.' We are afraid. We don't know *what* has happened. We ran all the way from the tomb to tell you and. . . ."

Peter and John had heard enough. They had to see for themselves. They ran down the outside staircase, through the narrow streets and to the grave. They found it just as the women had said. Indeed, the stone *had* been rolled away. When they went inside the tomb they found that it was—*empty!* Only the graveclothes were there. They did not know what to think.

More slowly, Mary Magdalene had followed the men running to the grave. Tears rolled down her cheeks. Arriving for the second time in the garden where Jesus had been buried, she saw Peter and John turn and leave. They were shaking their heads in amazement and despair.

After the men left, Mary Magdalene stooped and looked into the cave-like tomb herself. Sure enough, Jesus' body was not there!

As she turned to leave, she saw someone who she thought must be the gardener. "Why are you crying?" he said to her. The rising sun was in her eyes. She wiped her tears on the sleeve of her robe.

"Because they have taken away my Lord. If you have carried him away, sir, tell me where you have laid him."

"Mary," he said. "Mary, it is I."

"Teacher!" she exclaimed. "You are alive again! You have risen from the dead."

"Yes," said Jesus gently. "I am alive again. Go and tell my disciples."

Mary's tears turned to laughter and joy as she ran back to the city to share the good news. His body had not been stolen. Her Lord had risen from the dead. He had spoken to her and called her by her name. Soon he would appear to others also. Jesus, her Savior, was alive forevermore.

Chapter 11

With Jesus in the Breaking of Bread

Cleopas pounded on the door of the upper room where Jesus' disciples were hiding. It was after dark on Easter evening.

"Open up!" shouted Cleopas. "It is I, Cleopas. My wife and I have exciting news."

Inside the room Andrew fumbled with the bolt on the door. The disciples had been hiding since Jesus' crucifixion three days before. They were afraid the soldiers would arrest *them* next. Some other followers had now joined them.

"We have news, too," said Andrew as he opened the door. "The Lord is risen and has appeared to Peter!"

"I've seen him, too," added Mary Magdalene with excitement in her voice. "He spoke to me in the garden early this morning and called me by my name!"

"Then you will understand when we tell you

what happened to us. We were on our way from Jerusalem to our home in Emmaus when. . . ." Cleopas began, but his wife interrupted him.

"Let me tell it," she said. "We were on our way home and were talking about all the things that had happened to Jesus this past week. We talked about his triumphal entry last Sunday, his arrest by soldiers on Thursday, and finally his execution on a cross Friday. As we talked a stranger joined us and asked what we were talking about. 'Are you the only visitor to Jerusalem who has not heard of these things?' I asked him."

"Then the stranger began to talk to *us*," Cleopas broke in. "He said that the Messiah had had to suffer all these things to enter into his glory. He began to tell story after story about Moses and God's people long ago, and the prophets and how they were a part of God's plan. We had no idea who he was. Neither of us really looked at him. By this time we had reached the gate of our house. Since it was late we invited the stranger to join us for supper.

"At supper he took the loaf of bread, broke it, and gave each of us a piece. Now, somehow, we knew who was with us. We recognized him by the way he broke the bread, for we had eaten with him many times before. It was Jesus! But after a moment, we no longer saw him. He vanished."

"Yes," put in Cleopas' wife. "And we have hurried back here to tell you the news."

As they finished speaking, suddenly Jesus himself stood among them. No one had opened the door

for him. They had simply been eating together, and all of a sudden he was there!

"It's a ghost," exclaimed Philip. "No one could have come through that locked door." Everyone was frightened.

Jesus laughed. "Don't be afraid. It is I. Come over here and look at the wounds in my hands and in my side."

The followers and disciples were confused. It seemed too good to be true that Jesus was alive again.

"May I have something to eat?" Jesus asked.

Salome gave him some fish. He ate with them as he had done so many times before.

As Cleopas' wife sat there in the upstairs room with the disciples and other followers, she remembered the time when five thousand people had been with him—listening to him tell stories. It was late in the day and the people were hungry. Jesus had fed them all with only five loaves of bread and two fishes. On another occasion she had heard him say, "I am the bread of life." She had wondered at the time what that meant. Now she wondered again, *could that breaking of bread and eating with us have had some special kind of meaning?*

John was remembering something, too. He remembered the last supper he and the other disciples had eaten with Jesus before he was crucified. It had been in this very room.

"This is my body," Jesus had said as he broke the

loaf of bread. "Take—eat. Do this in remembrance of me."

And as Jesus had taken a drink from the cup he had said, "I will not drink again of the fruit of the vine until the kingdom comes."

Until the kingdom comes, thought John. *Here Jesus is eating and drinking with us once again—after his death and resurrection. Could it be that the kingdom is now beginning to come?* John wondered.

As the followers and Jesus ate and laughed and talked together that night, Jesus explained many things to them. He told them that the message of Moses, the prophets, and the Psalms had come true through his death and resurrection.

Following the resurrection of Jesus, the disciples and other followers never knew when the risen Lord might appear among them.

Once some of the disciples had been fishing all night and had caught nothing. Suddenly they looked up and saw through the early dawn light a man standing on the beach. He called to them.

"Have you caught anything?" shouted the man on the beach.

"Not a thing," they answered. "The fish just aren't here this morning."

"Then cast your net on the right side of the boat," said the man on the shore. "You'll find some fish there."

They cast their net on the other side as the

stranger had suggested and caught so many fish they could hardly pull the net in.

"It's the Lord!" shouted John. He had recognized his Master.

With that Peter jumped into the water to swim to shore. Some weeks before, when Jesus had been arrested, Peter had been so afraid that he had pretended he didn't even know Jesus at all. But now he was no longer afraid. He swam as fast as he could to the shore to be with his Lord.

When Peter waded up onto the beach, he found Jesus already had built a charcoal fire and had bread for them.

"Bring some of the fish you men have caught,"

said Jesus, "and we will all have breakfast together."

As the disciples and Jesus ate, Peter had a strange kind of peace. After that meal with him, Peter knew that Jesus had forgiven him.

They saw him one last time high on a hillside outside Jerusalem.

"We know now that you are the king. Is this the time for us to conquer the world for you?" asked John.

"Don't worry about the schedule. Leave that to God. But I do have a job for you to do," replied Jesus.

"Well, let's get started," exclaimed Peter. "What are we waiting for? Let's begin right now doing whatever you tell us to do."

"No, Peter, not yet. First the Holy Spirit must come to you and you will receive power. Then you are to be my witnesses in Jerusalem and in Judea and Samaria and to the ends of the earth. And remember, I will be with you always."

When Jesus had said this, he lifted up his hands and blessed the disciples. Then he ascended into heaven. They would never again see him in quite the same way.

They returned to the upper room. There the disciples, the women, and other followers joined in prayer and in songs of praise.

"What do you suppose Jesus meant when he said the Holy Spirit would come?" asked Joanna.

"I don't know what he meant, Joanna," said Mary, Jesus' own mother, putting her arm around the younger woman. "But I know that it must be something wonderful, and we must wait for it to happen. I believe it will happen soon."

"In the meantime," said Matthew, "I know that Jesus is with us always."

Chapter 12

The Church Is Born

Twelve-year-old Tamar could hardly make her way through the crowded streets of Jerusalem. She and the other servants with her had been given time off from their work in the household of Caiaphas, the High Priest, because this was a holiday — Pentecost.

Jews from everywhere had come to Jerusalem to celebrate. This was an ancient festival that came fifty days after Passover. It was a time of thanksgiving not only for the harvest, but also for the "law of Moses" that God's people had received so many centuries before.

Thousands of people swarmed in the streets. Roman soldiers were everywhere as they tried to control the crowd. Tamar noticed a family of dark-skinned people from Africa who spoke to one another in Egyptian.

She saw a man who seemed to be a professor from Athens. He was speaking in Greek to some young people. She heard a man from Rome talking to his wife in Latin. She saw a rich merchant who wore a colorful turban. She guessed his strange words must be Persian. Faithful Jews had come from near and far to worship and praise God.

Suddenly, Tamar heard a loud commotion. It came from the upper room of a house nearby.

"Listen to those people up there," said one of the other servants. "They really are celebrating their holiday. They are already drunk, and it is only 9 o'clock in the morning."

Just then several men rushed out the door onto the flat roof, down the stairs, and into the crowd in the street. The men were all talking at once. Tamar wasn't sure what language they spoke. One of them climbed onto a low wall and held up his hands to quiet the crowd. She heard him say, "We are not drunk. God has poured the Holy Spirit upon us."

"Who is that man?" Tamar asked a woman beside her. "He looks familar to me."

"His name is Peter," the woman answered with irritation. "Be quiet. I want to hear what he has to say."

Tamar heard Peter say, "The prophet Joel promised, 'God will pour out the Holy Spirit on all people—on young people, old people, men, and women. God's Spirit will come upon all who call on the name of the Lord, and they will be saved.' Today this is coming true."

Tamar did not wait to hear more. Peter seemed to be beginning to preach a sermon, and listening to a sermon was not the way she wanted to spend her holiday! She elbowed her way through the crowd, leaving her companions behind.

Tamar couldn't seem to forget the man who was preaching, however. Where had she seen him before? That question stayed on her mind as she wandered through the streets looking for adventure.

Several weeks later, Tamar was walking through the marketplace when she spied a friend.

"Rhoda," Tamar called to her. "I'm glad you are here. I've got to talk to someone. The strangest thing happened this morning just outside the Temple. When I was . . . well, it really started yesterday. . . ."

"Slow down, Tamar," interrupted Rhoda as she paid for fresh figs and placed them in her basket. "Start at the beginning." Rhoda, only fifteen herself and a maid in another household, had been a big sister to younger servant girls in the city.

"Yesterday afternoon," Tamar rushed on with her story, "I went to the Temple to pray. You remember the crippled man Ezra who is always begging there by the gate? Well, he was in his usual place. Two men came by and he asked them for money in his usual way.

"One of the men said, 'I don't have any money, but I give you what I do have. In the name of Jesus, walk.'

"He lifted Ezra to his feet, and Ezra could walk! He walked right into the Temple with the two men, jumping up and down and praising God. . . . That older man looked familiar to me."

"That's not so strange," said Rhoda. "I imagine the men were Peter and John, two of Jesus' disciples. I see them often. The house where I work, the home of Mary the mother of John Mark, has become a kind of headquarters for the followers of Jesus. Peter is the older man. He and John have had the power to heal ever since. . . ."

"So those men were disciples of Jesus. That explains it! That is why this Peter looked so familiar. I had seen him the night Jesus was arrested! While Jesus' trial was going on in Caiaphas' house where I work, Peter was in the courtyard. I knew he must be one of the disciples, and I said so. But Peter denied it. Three times he denied it! He was such a coward that night. He was afraid he would be arrested, too. I saw him run away and cry. . . . But today he was a different man."

"Go on with your story, Tamar. What else happened at the Temple? What makes you say Peter was so different?"

"Well, after Ezra was healed, Peter began to preach about Jesus. As he preached, the Temple guards arrested him and his partner. They put them in jail. This morning there was a trial. I listened from an adjoining room. Peter wasn't afraid of anything today! He knew he might be whipped or even put to death, but he and John talked about Jesus just the same. 'I must obey God rather than men,' Peter said.

"The judges decided to let them go free this time, though. But they warned them never to preach about Jesus any more or they would be arrested and beaten and maybe even killed. As I looked at those two men I knew they had no intention of keeping silent. I never saw such courage. They seemed filled with some strange kind of power."

"Oh, they were filled with power all right," Rhoda replied. "There is no doubt about it. On the day of Pentecost, as the followers of Jesus prayed in the upper room of the house where I work, something happened. Everyone in the room, men and women, young and old alike, were filled with the Holy Spirit. I was not in the room myself, but some who were there say it was like a mighty wind rushing through the room. Others said it was like tongues of fire descending on each one of them. Nobody seemed to describe the experience in the same way. Peter and others went outside to preach to the crowd in the street. People from many countries heard the words of the gospel, and they could all understand.

"They say that three thousand people believed that day. Men, women, and children, not only from here in Jerusalem but from other places and countries, were baptized and received the Holy Spirit. Others have been added to the group every day as the disciples continue to preach the Good News."

Tamar's mind was still on other things. "I wonder what made Peter so different? Today he was a

changed person from the man I saw a few weeks ago."
She said her thoughts aloud.

"Oh, Tamar!" Rhoda almost shouted, "You
haven't heard a word I've said. But come with me the
first of next week, and I'll show you what's going on."

At daybreak the following Sunday, Tamar and
Rhoda entered the large upper room in the house
where Rhoda worked. "The Lord is risen," was the
greeting from the Apostle John as they came in. "The
Lord is risen, indeed," Rhoda replied. Tamar saw that
the followers were seated at tables and eating
together.

"Come over here and join us, Tamar." She was
surprised to see one of her friends—a servant who
had been with her on the day of Pentecost.

"Tamar," her friend said, "I want you to meet
Salome."

Tamar was startled to see her servant friend
sitting beside a woman whose silk dress showed she
was very wealthy.

"This," her friend continued, "is Claudius. He
came here from Rome at Pentecost and has stayed to
learn more about Jesus." There was also at the table a
member of the high court. She remembered having
heard him call for the death sentence for Jesus the
night of the trial. Now he was a believer! *How strange!*
she thought. *Even some of the religious leaders have become
a part of this fellowship.*

Someone at the table began to sing a psalm.
Others joined in.

One after the other, disciples told of things Jesus had said and done among them. They told how Jesus had received the Spirit when he was baptized. They told of people Jesus had healed through the power of that Holy Spirit and of his feeding the hungry. They told of his saying that followers should give away all they had to follow him. They recalled that Jesus' message of the kingdom was one that included people of every culture and country in the world. And they always spoke of the cross and of the resurrection.

Peter told about his own trial, which Tamar had seen. "We cannot be silent," he said, "no matter what they do to us. We must tell the world about Jesus. I thank God that I am counted worthy to suffer for my Lord. No matter what they do to me, I will preach about Jesus."

What a strange way to talk, thought Tamar, *thanking God for a chance to suffer!*

Tamar noticed that followers were giving money to the disciples. "What are they doing *that* for?" she whispered to Rhoda. "Is there some kind of 'tax' for belonging to the group?"

"Oh, no," explained Rhoda. "Followers give because they want to. See that man over there? His name is Barnabas. He owned a very valuable piece of land. He sold it and gave all the money to be used to help others. This is what Jesus told us to do. No one of us is either rich or poor. In this fellowship we have all things in common. We especially help those who cannot help themselves."

Peter stood to pray. He lifted both hands as he thanked God for those from other countries who heard and believed on the day of Pentecost and had taken the Good News to other parts of the world. And he asked God to give them courage to witness even if they should be thrown in prison, whipped, beaten—or even killed.

Tamar began to feel a strange kind of peace and joy come over her. She was seeing in others something she wanted, too. *Perhaps*, she thought, *I, too, am beginning to receive the Holy Spirit.*

She left Rhoda and the others at the table and went over to Peter.

"Peter," she said, "I first saw you the night Jesus was arrested. I am a maid for Caiaphas, the high priest. I knew you were a disciple that night and said so to you. But you denied it. Now you've changed. You are no longer afraid.

"I have changed, too," she said. "I believe in Jesus and want to be baptized and become a part of the church. I know it will not be easy. I may get into trouble back at Caiaphas' house where I work. But I want to be a follower of Jesus, too."

Peter put his strong arm around her. Tamar was about the age of his own daughter, who was there in the room, too.

"I will baptize you myself, my child," he said. "The risen Christ is giving the Holy Spirit to all God's people everywhere. You are receiving that Spirit, too."

117

Glossary

baptism—the act of sprinkling with or dipping a person in water as a sign of washing away sin and of the coming of the Holy Spirit.

Caesar—the title of the Roman emperor in Jesus' day. Rome had conquered the Jews.

Calvary—the place outside the Jerusalem wall where Jesus was crucified.

caravan—a group traveling together, often merchants or pilgrims.

centurion—a commander of one hundred soldiers in the Roman army.

covenant—a solemn promise; an agreement between God and God's people.

crucifixion (crucify)—a way Romans punished criminals by nailing them to crosses and leaving them to die.

disciple—a follower; a learner.

Holy Spirit—the Spirit of God.

hosanna—Hebrew word for "save us."

Kingdom of God—the rule of God in the lives of people.

Lamb of God—a title for Jesus, the Messiah— implying that he would die for our sins.

Last Supper—the supper shared with the disciples in the upper room the night before Jesus was crucified.

Levite—an official helper of the priests.

manger—a box in a barn from which horses or cattle eat.

Messiah—the promised one to be anointed King of the Jews.

money changer—a person through whom a worshipper had to exchange her or his money for the kind of coins used for offerings in the Temple.

Mount of Olives—a mountain just outside Jerusalem.

oasis—a place in the desert where there are trees, water, and grass.

Passover—the annual feast in memory of the escape of God's people from Egypt in the time of Moses.

Pentecost—the Jewish thanksgiving feast of harvest. On this day seven weeks after Easter the Holy Spirit came to the apostles.

Pharisees—a group of Jews who were *very* strict in keeping the laws of Moses.

priest—a religious leader who performed ceremonial duties as a part of worship.

prophet—a person who preaches what God has revealed to her or him.

rabbi—a Jewish teacher of God's law.

Religious Council (also called Sanhedrin)—the supreme court of the Jews in Jesus' day.

repent—to be sorry for having done wrong and to seek to change and be forgiven.

Sabbath—a day of the week used for rest and worship—beginning on Friday at sundown and ending Saturday as the first stars appear.

sacrifice—to give up something, often as a part of worship. Frequently this involved killing a lamb.

Sadducees—a religious and political party much less strict than the Pharisees. They often compromised with the Romans.

salvation—deliverance from sin; God's gift of a better life.

Sanhedrin—see Religious Council.

Samaritans—inhabitants of the province of Samaria, whom Jews in Jesus' day looked down on and hated.

Satan—the evil spirit, the opposite of goodness, the devil.

savior—deliverer; one who saves from trouble, oppression, or sin.

scribe—a teacher and copier of Jewish law.

sin—to break the law of God; to live for self, not God.

Son of God—Messiah, the promised king.

swaddling clothes—strips of cloth that were used in Jesus' day to wrap newborn babies.

synagogue—a group of Jews who gather for worship; also used for the place where they worship.

temple—a building used for worship.

temptation—a test of one's loyalty to God.

Zealots—a political party of Jews plotting a violent revolt against the Romans who ruled them.

MAPS

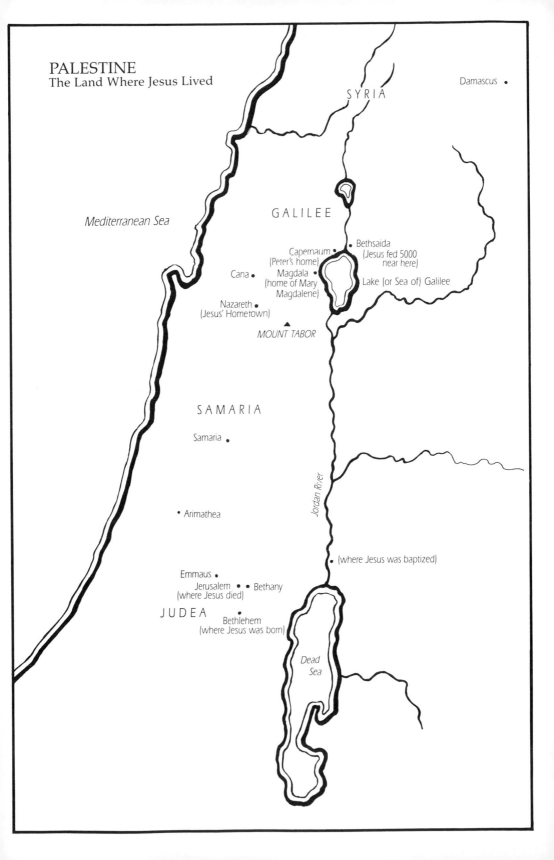

PALESTINE
The Land Where Jesus Lived

SYRIA

Damascus •

Mediterranean Sea

GALILEE

• Bethsaida
Capernaum • (Jesus fed 5000
(Peter's home)   near here)
Cana •   Magdala •
(home of Mary   Lake (or Sea of) Galilee
Magdalene)
Nazareth •
(Jesus' Hometown)
▲
MOUNT TABOR

SAMARIA

Samaria •

Jordan River

• Arimathea

• (where Jesus was baptized)

Emmaus •
Jerusalem • • Bethany
(where Jesus died)
JUDEA
Bethlehem •
(where Jesus was born)

Dead
Sea